GERONTION

GERONTION

Alan Hill

HappenStance

ISBN 978-1-910131-26-8

Previous poetry by Alan Hill:

No Biography, Happen*Stance* Press, 2010
To Rocamadour, Redbeck Press, 2005
The Green Tide, Rivelin Press, 1975

Printed and bound in the UK by 4edge Limited, Essex

Published in 2016 by Happen*Stance*,
21 Hatton Green, Glenrothes, Fife KY7 4SD
Further info. from: nell@happenstancepress.com
www.happenstancepress.com

For all my old friends,
living and dead

~ I ~

SOMETHING IS WRONG. MY
barber knows my name, recalls
what I recall—but
as he cuts, the hair that falls
is white, not like mine at all.

~ II ~

I PULL A NEW LEAF
from my calendar each day,
watching the new year
grow thinner, while leaf by leaf
I throw my old life away.

~ III ~

MY FRIENDS AND I SIT
like elderly passengers
waiting for our planes.
When a flight is called, someone
rises quietly, and leaves.

~ IV ~

THAT IS A STRANGE DAY
when you wake to discover
age has drifted down
imperceptibly, like dust,
and you're totally covered.

~ V ~

MANY YEARS AGO
I wrote a worried letter
to a Minister.
Now it's been researched, and I'm
a footnote in history.

~ VI ~

GOBLINS AND GORGONS
beset all the passages
of an old man's world.
But the young don't fear them,
don't see them; walk straight
through them.

~ VII ~

QUIET AUTUMN DAYS.
I seem now mostly to be
made of memories
like old wounds, sometimes aching
according to the weather.

~ VIII ~

HEART YOU'VE SERVED ME WELL,
unceasingly beating for
seventy-eight years,
but sometimes stumbling now—
rehearsing your final bow?

~ IX ~

JUST THE OTHER NIGHT
I dreamed of her, for the first
time in fifty years.
She seemed well; young and happy.
I wonder if she has died?

~ X ~

MUTABILITY.
All is mutability,
and sometimes it seems
that there's no more to be said,
except perhaps entropy.

~ XI ~

THOSE CAN'T BE MY LEGS—
those purple-veined spindle-shanks,
knob-knees and ankles!
Could a *person* live in such
an absurd caricature?

~ XII ~

I KEEP LOSING WORDS.
They disappear between
brain and tongue, like coins
that fall and roll out of sight,
hiding for days. Even weeks.

~ XIII ~

WALKING DOWN HILL STREET
I passed by the premises
of *Prostate Scotland*—
a chill reminder. Would it
had been in some other street.

~ XIV ~

WHAT IS 'A SHILLING'?
she asked. But I couldn't bridge
the thousand-year gap
that had suddenly opened
between her world and my own.

~ XV ~

'DIFFERENT IN YOUR DAY
I suppose,' and the young man
smiled. Bloody cheek!
'I haven't died yet,' I said.
'While I live, it's *still* my day.'

~ XVI ~

AS THE DAY FADED
I stood for ages watching
a small golden cloud.
How strange to be a creature
that finds a cloud absorbing!

~ XVII ~

NOW, IN MY OLD AGE,
almost all that's in my head
belongs to the past.
No more long-term investments.
Let each day unfold itself.

~ XVIII ~

WAGNER'S RING CYCLE—
so very aptly titled.
Sixteen majestic
seemingly endless hours
of bum-numbing tedium.

~ XIX ~

OVER THE WEIR
like glass the bronze water slides.
Dreaming, we watch it
while the water flows past us
and the silent years glide by.

~ XX ~

WE ARE, AS OBJECTS,
subject to laws of matter
and laws of motion;
well-kent as the amoeba;
as unexplored as ocean.

~ XXI ~

I FART AS I WALK.
Forget tolerance, wisdom,
insight, peace of mind.
The reality of age
is this: you fart as you walk.

~ XXII ~

MOUTH, GUT AND ANUS!
At my age what else matters?
While they remain in
working order I can live
with remnants of enjoyment.

~ XXIII ~

WHO DOESN'T HOPE TO
startle the future with his
footprint in the sand?
But whose print is so deep that
no tide will wash it away?

~ XXIV ~

FOUR PEOPLE TALKING
of life's phases. One said he'd
planned out every stage.
Have I wasted eighty years
making each day a new page?

~ XXV ~

I TALK TO THE DEAD
continually—old friends,
colleagues, relations.
They smile a lot, nod, and
sometimes we laugh together.

~ XXVI ~

THE LAWS OF NATURE
sometimes combine to produce,
let's say, an iceberg.
Maybe even one for you.
The trick is not to hit it.

~ XXVII~

BEFORE THE BIG BANG
I was writing a treatise
about creation.
But as usual I was
overtaken by events.

~ XXVIII ~

ANOTHER CHRISTMAS—
the card to his widow for
the twenty-third year;
and sometimes, still, his silence
is all that I can hear.

~ XXIX ~

THE LOST PLACES—WOODS
felled, fields built on, houses
and streets demolished—
old songs that nobody sings.
But I still hum them sometimes.

~ XXX ~

HOW RELENTLESSLY
the earth continues to turn,
never, seemingly,
losing any momentum.
Today is no different.

~ XXXI ~

I HAVE JOLTED DOWN
one of those steps of ageing.
After two hours
of gardening yesterday
I can scarcely climb the stairs.

~ XXXII ~

I TAMPERED WITH TIME
today—stole an hour from
each clock in the house.
It made no difference. Time
compensates by speeding up.

~ XXXIII ~

REMEMBERING NOW
all those recommended texts
I failed to read,
I begin to understand
why I ought to have read them.

~ XXXIV ~

LIKE BEDIVERE
I hear the quiet reeds
rustle as they move
in the endless wind that blows
all day on an empty shore.

~ XXXV ~

IN A LINE WE COME,
moving to the pulse's drum,
hands linked all along.
Briefly silhouetted we
dance over time's horizon.

~ XXXVI ~

WE MUST ALL FOLLOW
the inescapable path
of the labyrinth,
into its empty centre,
where nothing is but oneself.

~ XXXVII ~

I AM IN THIS ROOM,
but don't know why I'm here.
Then I remember.
My feet know what I'm doing,
though my head doesn't seem to.

~ XXXVIII ~

I'VE NO PAINS TODAY!
Today I feel well, fit
and energetic,
quite like the old days. I could
tackle anything. Today.

~ XXXIX ~

MY FEET ARE SHRINKING!
Shoes that fitted slide about.
My brain's shrinking too!
Bugger me, what a prospect—
a pin-headed matchstick-man!

~ XL ~

IN ONE BRIEF SEASON,
from spring green to the yellow
leaf, we are sered.
Following hedgerow reason
Lad's Love is Old Man's Beard.

~ XLI ~

I CANNOT STAND AT
any high altar, nor pray
tall and confident;
but in some shadowed corner
may uncertainly murmur.

~ XLII ~

SIXTY YEARS AND MORE
this limestone fossil has lain,
silent, on my desk.
Where found, with whom, I recall
clearly; and what she said.

~ XLIII ~

FLESH FAILS, THINGS CHANGE;
even self itself falters
and fades into mist.
Love and gold will endure.
But love's better. Love listens.

~ XLIV ~

I WRITE THESE BRIEF LINES
like messages in bottles,
floating out on time,
giving my co-ordinates,
and wondering about yours.

~ XLV ~

THE SCENT OF A ROSE
brings back my father's garden,
ripe plums to be picked,
and the pages of life's book
wonderfully unwritten.

~ XLVI ~

RHYTHM AND BLUES MAN?
Yes, you could say so, but now
that I'm older it's
the rhythm of the seasons,
and quiet blues when friends die.

~ XLVII ~

IN THIS DARK SILENCE
it seems that all the world sleeps,
while—unquiet—
I stand here listening
to the distance of the stars.

~ XLVIII~

AT SCHOOL I WAS TAUGHT
about moments of force, and
I've found them useful.
Now, though, I'm learning about
the quiet force of moments.

~ XLIX~

I DIDN'T MISS HIM,
although his mind was clouded
and we didn't meet.
But he died a year since, and
now I miss him constantly.

~ L ~

AT MY TABLE NOW
I keep constant company
with the Grim Reaper.
We converse aimiably,
but he gives nothing away.

~ LI ~

GROANING HELPS. STIFFENED
upper lips impress, suggest
classical learning,
though don't abate pain. But yes,
groaning definitely helps.

~ LII ~

WHILE MULLING OVER
some eternal verities
I was distracted
by a painful toenail.
I suppose that's one of them.

~ LIII ~

WRINKLED RETINA!
Now I live in a hall of
distorting mirrors.
Chimneys shimmy like *houris*
and every steeple's crooked.

~ LIV ~

I SHALL TAKE A FEW
secrets to the grave with me
and I'm glad of it.
Some things are better taken
from the world. I can do that.

~ LV ~

WHEN MY HANDS WERE DEFT,
my step quick, my spirits high,
I would sometimes rage.
Now, in blunt-fingered age I'm
often more inclined to sigh.

~ LVI ~

ON A PILGRIMAGE
it's the getting there that counts.
Insights and blessings
we carry within us; it's
the journeying calls them out.

~ LVII~

SO MANY OLD FRIENDS
and people I've been fond of
have died this winter.
The music is still playing,
but very few chairs are left.

~ LVIII ~

SHY AS A DEER,
what might be a poem stirs
at the edge of sight.
Be still. Be quiet. Let it
think itself unseen. Then write.

~ LIX ~

I WAS NOT PREPARED
for his sudden death although
he was eighty-five.
You get so used to living
you forget it has to stop.

~ LX ~

ZEN GARDEN: GRAVEL
smoothed around immobile rocks.
Pattern is meaning.
Petals fall. Thought is constant.
Now. Be silent. Be still. Be.